MW01073727

Landmark
insights.
Book 5

Creating a Future You Really Want

Published by
Landmark Worldwide
353 Sacramento St., Ste. 200
San Francisco, CA 94111

ISBN-13: 978-0692148143
ISBN-10: 0692148140

Printed in the United States of America
First Edition

This book points out what is possible if we step outside of what we know, and recognize and embrace our capacity to bring forth an entirely new possibility for living—not because it is better, but simply because that is what human beings can do.

Engaging in Something Bigger than Ourselves

Everything in our own immediate experience supports the notion that we are the center of the universe. The world is there in front of US or behind US, to the left or right of US. Other people's thoughts and feelings have to be communicated to us somehow, but ours are so immediate, urgent, real.[1]

Wherever we are located in the world, we essentially refer to ourselves always as "here," and things *other than ourselves*, always as "there." Seeing ourselves as located in-here, and all else out-there is a built-in default orientation, placing us in one sense as bystanders, to our lives.

Often we think of "I" as that which goes on with us internally (our attitudes and moods, feelings, emotions, thoughts, bodily sensations, etc.) Other times we think of "I" through a filter of some theory, idea, memory, belief, etc. Stopping at either of those default places, however, doesn't allow us to investigate the full panoply available in being human. It's not that we want to leave behind that whole gestalt, rather we want to hold that whole world of feelings, theories, etc. in a different way, so that they illuminate (vs. limit) what we encounter day to day.

Transforming our relationships with ourselves, each other, and the world requires a radical departure from our default orientation. When we're fully engaged in something larger than ourselves, it turns out that what's going on with us internally has very little primacy. Rather than being limited by who we've considered ourselves to be, opportunities for *being* and *acting* powerfully show themselves. When we recognize that the world, the communities that make it up, and what we refer to as "I" are in fact not *in-here*, but out "on the court," of life, we have the freedom to choose a richer and more expansive game. And it's there that we're called upon to meet the call of a possibility bigger than ourselves.

Relationships: A Stand We Take for Another

The profound love that's possible in our relationships comes from a deep sense of alignment—an alignment of vision, of our most fundamental intentions and purpose(s) in life, in which each person knows there's a space for the other to be, to exist, to grow, to flourish. Relationships are a creative act, a commitment that lives in action—a stand we take for someone.

When doubts, considerations, or disagreements occur, they aren't in opposition, or contrary to that stand—but an invitation to dance with what's in front of us. It's not the content (the circumstances or the "what happened") in our relationships that determines their quality and power or keeps them from being great—it's the way we "hold" that content. If, however, we find ourselves just complaining (about *what's missing* in our relationship or *what's there* that we don't want there) as if *not being satisfied* "is" our stand, that's a pretty useful thing to recognize about ourselves. How powerful are a person's actions when those actions are the product of complaint? To promise to provide what's missing leaves us at risk; to complain we have no risk at all. It's in risking ourselves—in revealing ourselves to one another—that we become ourselves.

There are no facts that limit the possibility of our relationships, there are only *conversations* that limit or *conversations* that create possibility. We have a choice about what's at play. Relationships are something we bring forth as a declaration—a stand we take for another.

Being Fully Ourselves—The Courage to Live in a Transformed Way

Having power, success, and freedom is a lot more risky than not having them. This business about freedom, about power, is really a product of a place to stand. It takes courage to live in a transformed way—to give up mediocrity, to live consistent with what we know is possible, even when there's nothing urgent at stake. If we find ourselves "settling for less" from time-to-time and can see that as an invention, *a matter of saying*, it affords us a larger opening—power and freedom are ours again.

Being fully ourselves always wants to happen in us and requires our active participation. It's not something out in front of us that we're working on, or measuring ourselves against. It's not predictive, not a "get-to" thing—it's declarative, a "come-from" thing, a place to stand, *a matter of saying*. Our ideals, standards, and expectations occur in language. Our reluctance, accommodation, and powerlessness occur in language. Yet language is the home, the only home of possibility. If anything creative is going to show up in life, the domain in which it shows up is the stand for its possibility, like a real action in life.

"*The pay is actually about the same.*"

Forgiveness Enlarges the Future

Forgiveness is one of the most powerful actions a human being can take—it doesn't change the past, it enlarges the future.[2] Forgiveness is a choice that frees us from the burden of resentment and regret—it doesn't alter the past, make things right, condone what we did or may have been done to us. It shifts the present and allows us to move forward. Creating a new future is declarative and takes a commitment to being complete with those involved.

Forgiveness isn't really about the person who we say has done wrong. It's about the one who is forgiving. It's about finding the courage to step out of "the way it should have been." To complete a past hurt, resentment, or anger it's worth noticing how we're holding what happened now, as well as recognizing that whatever happened more than likely will have gained over time a certain mass and complexity in our minds. In taking that into account, we're more able to address the context, hear others, and look at what might be next. For example, if we're harboring resentment, it involves taking responsibility for the diminishment of the other person and requires generative language, such as "I'm giving up the grudge I've been harboring for years." Upsets and grudges we carry from the past narrow our options, impact our relationships, and limit our experience of living fully.

If resentment and anger stay with us, circumstances have the power, not us. Forgiveness puts the power fully in our hands. It creates a space in which a new future can be created, and points to the capacity we have to reach out beyond ourselves.

Possibility Leaves Us with Power and Freedom

All we are given is possibilities—to make of ourselves one thing or another.
    —Ortega y Gasset

An "expectation unfulfilled" or "ideal unfulfilled" leads to a lack of power, where a "possibility unfulfilled" leads to a possibility—and no loss of power or freedom. When we look at our experience vs. what we'd hoped for or how we thought things would go (but it didn't turn out that way), then go out and create a new possibility, it can feel like that's against a backdrop that negates it. It doesn't occur to us as something's "missing like a possibility," it occurs more like an invalidation or that something's wrong—like there's something we feel we need to justify or defend. In getting stuck there, we miss out on that place of power and freedom.

The domain of possibility doesn't exist; we need to create it in order for it to exist. (Happiness, fulfillment, regard, satisfaction are all states that exist only as a *possibility*. So is everything else that's of any value.) We can't have power and freedom because we want it, because it would be good to have, because it would make life better or easier, or because we would succeed with it. What gives power and freedom is to live in a "possibility" that calls for power and freedom. A possibility truly is "to be" that something is possible. There are no facts that limit possibility there are only conversations that limit or create possibility. Language shapes the way we think, the way we live our lives, and it gives us hands-on access to a world that's open to being invented.

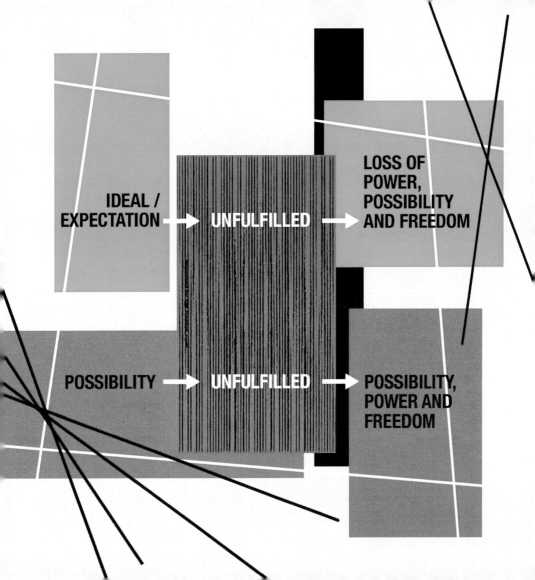

Being Fully at Home with Ourselves

Our "identity," *who we consider ourselves to be*, is essentially arrived at by default, assembled to adapt to something we saw as *wrong* or some seeming insufficiency. Mostly when we were young and learning to deal with life, we made decisions to get through the circumstances we encountered. Those decisions worked at the time, so we kept them around, inadvertently defining *who we are* today, and leaving us with a subtle but disconcerting inability to be fully at home with ourselves.

A kind of absurdity lies in acting as if who we are today is a compilation of those ways of being we put together way back then. Once our "identity" is seen for what it is, it becomes clear that it's not fixed or set and we're not in any way stuck with those ways of being. Stepping outside of our identity, however, isn't so easy, as our identity has achieved a certain density throughout our lives. In recognizing that *who we consider ourselves to be* is not an absolute, we reveal what's possible in being human—giving us hands-on access to a world that's malleable and open to being invented.

"I wish my identity weren't so wrapped up with who I am."

In Inventing Ourselves, the Way the World Occurs Shifts

In our relationships, when we focus on our problems or how wrong things are, we lose our power to be and act effectively. Problems lie in the lack of inventing a future for our relationships "as a possibility." When there's no possibility created, pretty much what's left is being upset. The payoff in that is that we get to be right and see others as wrong. In being upset, in withholding our happiness and well-being, we both limit the other person as well as our own ability to be. If we switch that, if we *invent ourselves* (instead of just reacting), the way the world occurs shifts—we could be in a relationship with Godzilla, or anyone. If we don't switch that, we don't get a chance to celebrate all that's available to ourselves and others.

When something's *missing as a possibility*, there's not a sense of insufficiency or inadequacy—we leave behind the conversation about how things are "not" going to be. *What's missing* becomes a possibility "for" something. Making this switch requires disrupting our old conversations and most likely completing things from the past—there's no wish for things to be different, better, or more. We come to know a space within ourselves where that can happen—it's a state change, to being the author, as it were. The conditions and circumstances for our relationships begin to reorder and realign themselves. In creating possibility, we get to know what's possible in being human.

Shifting the Horizon of What's Possible

We often approach life counting on a certain *order of things*, thinking that predictability and control are possible. Then we encounter the experience of uncertainty, often with chaos close on its heels. This ambiguity and randomness can sometimes be disconcerting, as we don't readily see an effective way of being related to it. Sometimes we'd drift toward dealing with things rationally, sometimes emotionally. Neuroscientist David Eagleman captures the duality: *"There is an ongoing conversation among the different factions in [our] brain, each competing to control the single output channel of [our] behavior. The rational system is one that cares about the analysis of things in the outside world, while the emotional system monitors the internal state...."*

Because we don't see a ready way to relate powerfully with these dual realities, we attempt to apply patterns of order—and the more we do that, the less effective we become. It's like trying to be an artist by the numbers—the better we get at that, the worse our art is. Predictability and control are irrelevant to the phenomenon of possibility. There is no certainty as an *inevitability* or predictability of an outcome. *We* are the ones saying something is possible. Real power occurs when we know we have something to say about the way things are. Recognizing that shifts the horizon of what's possible, and it's from there the full range available in being human can be explored and lived.

ETCHING: RICHARD TUTTLE, *LABLE 13*, *LABLE 13*, 2004-5, FROM A SERIES OF 16 ETCHINGS ENTITLED CLOTH (*LABLE 1-16*). PUBLISHED BY BROOKE ALEXANDER, INC., NEW YORK

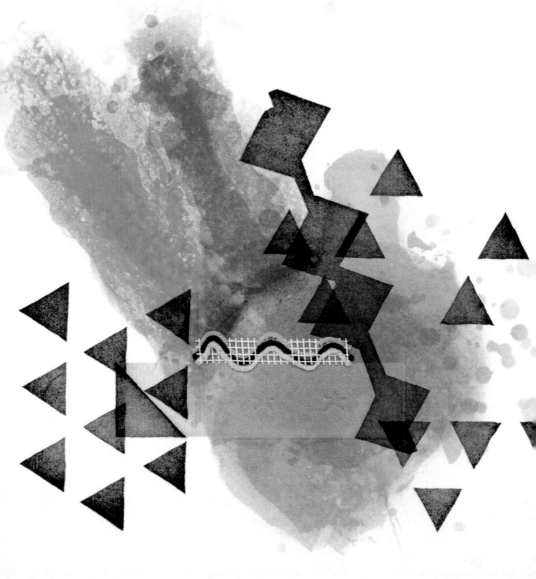

The Power to Choose Is Uniquely Human

Decisions have to be made constantly. Coin-flipping, I Ching consultation, Rock-Paper-Scissors, asking a friend are all time-honored means of coming to a decision… What should I be for Halloween? Is New Zealand a good place to retire? Who should I vote for? What clothes should I buy?[3]

How to live a life based on possibility in a world where possibility regularly defaults to deciding amongst options, predictability, and forecasting…? Options are familiar, foreseeable extrapolations, essentially forecasts based on our past interpretations. Ironically, however, they're just *repetitions in disguise*, not really options at all, leaving us with our old interpretations determining our future. *Choice* is another matter—it's the profoundly human ability to create.

In recognizing that whatever interpretations we made "way back when" were in fact a choice, we begin to see ourselves as authors of those interpretations, and come into the immense freedom of a whole new domain. This is the domain of possibility, brought into being by declaration, by invention, by our *saying*. When choice is known in this way, what previously seemed simply part of "the way things are" shows up differently. When we transform our approach to life from the two-dimensional sort of living (a past/present circularity) to a three-dimensional freedom that includes the *creation of possibility* another world becomes available. The power to choose is uniquely human—instead of a process of selecting and strategizing among existing options, the nature of possibility emerges, with all the power and efficacy that accompany it.

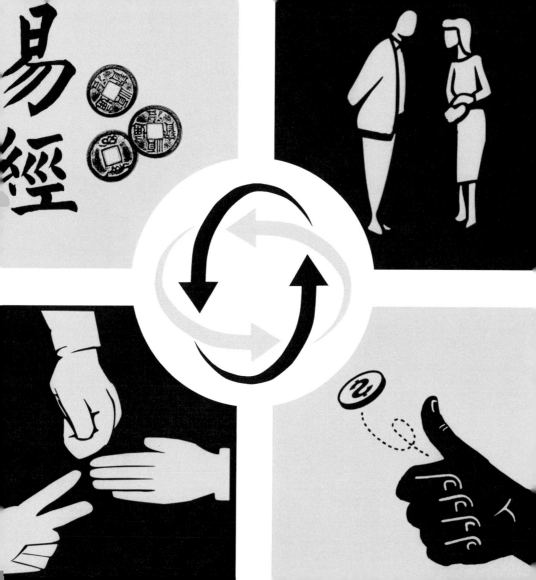

The Vastness of What's Available in Being Human

Two mirrors facing each other create a fun-house hall that ricochets an image back and forth until it vanishes into an infinite regress. If we placed a chameleon in that hall, it would try to disappear in a universe of itself—endlessly cycling through a number of its disguises. The very act of accommodating itself to its own reflection would disturb it anew.[4]

Early in life, in certain situations, we might feel judged or compare ourselves to others and think we come up short in some way, etc., and feel that "something's wrong." In those moments, we decide that we don't have what it takes to "win" in life. To compensate, we figure out a *way of being* (a "strong suit" or "strategy for winning" so to speak) to address whatever we think of as missing. Those early decisions become far-reaching declarations that set the stage for our world view, essentially our whole future. We then set out to hone those *ways of being*. Once honed, they become fixed, a permanent part of our identity (who we consider ourselves to be). When we meet similar situations, no matter how many years later, those strategies get triggered and the *infinite* regress kicks in.

In recognizing that whatever interpretations we made "way back when" were in fact a choice, we begin to see ourselves as authors of those interpretations, and we come into the immense freedom of a whole new domain—*the domain of possibility*, brought into being by our *saying*.

ILLUSTRATION: MANOUK VAN EESTEREN

Manouk van Eesteren

Breakthroughs are Brought Forth, Created, Generated—Spoken First as Possibility

Breakthroughs begin with holding a picture of *what if, what might, what could be.* Breakthroughs aren't something we make, because to make something is to take what's there and change it—a breakthrough is to take what *isn't* and have it *be.* A breakthrough is a discontinuous result—being someplace without having covered the distance between where we started and where we wound up. Breakthroughs allow for sudden powerful insights that take us past our self-imposed limitations. Breakthroughs alter our sense of who we are, alter the quality of our life, alter being alive.

We don't give the idea of breakthroughs a whole lot of thought—we mostly focus on the day-to-day business of living. If we get stopped or stuck along the way, we naturally attempt to figure out *more, better, or different scenarios* to accomplish what we are after, but most often do so within the same framework, leading only to incremental improvements. Given, however, that both *what we're engaged* with and *how things occur for us* are shaped by language, we have the power to author and alter our lives. Language gives us direct access to ourselves, to who we are, to creating possibility— not possibility like options, but possibility like the boundless dimension that's added to the world by the human ability to create.

WHAT IF, WHAT MIGHT, WHAT WILL BE?

What We Have to Offer Each Other is Ourselves—Our Listening, and Our Speaking

We are essentially in conversations with ourselves most of the time—how we listen is determined by our "concerns" (being successful, being liked, wanting to know "what's in it" for us, how things will turn out, etc.). That voiceover, is not necessarily bad—it's just that we don't really hear the other person, or they us. What we're saying to others, or they to us, might seep in from time to time, but it isn't in what we or they are saying—it's what we're saying plus what they are saying about what we're saying, which isn't what we're saying, vice versa. That dynamic has us miss out on the full possibility of communication—and the infinite worlds it makes available.

Listening without the filters of those concerns has enormous power. Listening is the clearing in which speaking can occur—it's the possibility for understanding, for meaning, for being known and loved. Speaking is what allows for *who* and *how we are* in the world. It's what allows for the futures we create, where our ideas become clear and possible, where we share ourselves, and where others are expanded by our participation with them. Speaking and listening are not just something we do in response to a world that exists outside of us—they're what brings that very world into being—it's through language that life really happens. When we see language this way—as that which gives rise to the world and that which gives access to what is in that world—it alters the very nature of what's possible. When we look at what it is we have to offer each other, it's only ourselves—our listening, and our speaking.

Freedom—A Matter of Choosing, A Place to Stand

We commonly think of freedom as the ability to define options and choose among them. The context or framework inside which we talk about freedom is freedom "from," freedom "of," freedom "to." But in the possibility of being human, there is a freedom that is distinct from the freedoms "from," "of," and "to." The word *freedom* carries *choice*. Freedom is a matter of choosing. While freedom can be defined, it can't be captured or corralled by a definition—it leaks out when we try to define it. Freedom is closer to *being* than it is to some *thing*. It's kind of a *being* phenomenon.

In our commitments—the places we've chosen to find ourselves in life—lies the freedom we have. When we commit ourselves to our partners, families, projects, service, those commitments become a freedom—we recognize our ultimate choice and responsibility. Freedom is a product of a place to stand. What we say to ourselves and about ourselves shapes our possibilities for being. Taking a stand requires an act of *courage*, and a willingness to be shaped and moved by our commitments—that's where freedom arises. When we take a stand we don't have to take the stand out into the world of black and white, yes or no, accomplished or did not accomplish. That isn't where the courage is. The courage is where the stand meets the commitment.

a matter of choosing a place to stand

Pleasure Disappoints, Possibility Never

If I were to wish for anything I should not wish for wealth and power, but for the passionate sense of what can be—for the eye, which, ever young and ardent, sees the possible. Pleasure disappoints, possibility never. And what wine is so sparkling, what so fragrant, what so intoxicating as possibility? [5]

It's the phenomenon of possibility itself that brings about breakdowns. When we create a possibility, we create a new context, and when that possibility is big enough, the reality we're currently living doesn't match up with the new context. There's a gap, that gap starts to create breakdowns, and we experience what's happening now as inconsistent with the possibility. If we hadn't created a possibility that took us beyond where we were, there would be no experience of a breakdown.

We disempower ourselves in dealing with breakdowns when we entertain conversations about *what's wrong.* The minute the conversation becomes about what's wrong, we try to fix and/or change what we see as wrong, and lose the possibility we created. Why? Because the possibility we created can't exist inside "something's wrong" or inside the "solution to a problem."

How do we get the possibility back? In recognizing that what's happening is a breakdown, we can return to a conversation for possibility; restore, recreate, and regenerate that possibility; and take actions to fulfill the possibility. We become a powerful opening for action—we get to know what's possible in being human.

PLEASURE DISAPPOINTS, POSSIBILITY NEVER.

Endnotes

1. Adapted from David Foster Wallace, *Commencement Speech* (Kenyon University, 2005).

2. Adapted from Paul Boese (*Quote Magazine*, 19 February 1967).

3. Adapted from Cory Doctorow (boing boing, 15 June 2009).

4. Adapted from Kevin Kelly, *Out of Control* (Basic Books, 1995).

5. Kierkegaard

Made in United States
North Haven, CT
20 October 2023

42971175R00020